FICTION 🪶 MRS. WARREN'S HOUSE

Written by Katherine Rawson
Illustrated by Ann Caranci

Chapter 1	Five Boring Months	2
Chapter 2	Through the Window	4
Chapter 3	Filling the Feeder	8
Chapter 4	Tasha's Garden	14

PIONEER VALLEY EDUCATIONAL PRESS, INC.

CHAPTER 1 FIVE BORING MONTHS

Tasha wished she could go home after school, but ever since her mother got a new job, she had to spend her afternoons at Mrs. Warren's house. And Mrs. Warren's house was the most boring place in the world.

Mrs. Warren was nice. She always came to the door with a smile and a cookie. But she was ancient. She didn't know any games. After Tasha ate her snack, there was nothing for them to do. They just sat by the window until Tasha's mother picked her up.

Tasha couldn't wait for summer. In the summer,
she would go to camp with her friends.
But summer was still five months away.
Five months in Mrs. Warren's boring, old house.

CHAPTER 2 THROUGH THE WINDOW

The snow was melting. Little buds were starting to bloom on Mrs. Warren's tree.

Spring was on its way, but Tasha didn't care. She just stared through Mrs. Warren's window and dreamed of swimming with her friends.

One day, something in the tree captured Tasha's attention. It looked like a tube stuck to a plate.

"What's that thing?" she asked.

"That's the bird feeder," said Mrs. Warren. "You fill it with seeds." She sighed. "I used to love observing the birds when they'd fly in for a snack."

"Why don't you put seeds in it anymore?" asked Tasha.

"I'd like to," said Mrs. Warren, "but it's hard for me to go out in the cold."

"Doesn't that make you sad?" asked Tasha.

"It's OK," said Mrs. Warren. "It makes me happy just to remember them."

That afternoon, as Tasha looked out the window, she felt sad for Mrs. Warren.

"Maybe she misses the birds the same way I miss my mom and my friends," she thought.

CHAPTER 3 • FILLING THE FEEDER

The next afternoon, Tasha told Mrs. Warren, "I could fill the feeder for you."

"That would be very nice," said Mrs. Warren. "I think the seeds are still on the porch."

Mrs. Warren showed Tasha how to pour the seeds into the feeder.

"What if squirrels eat it all?" asked Tasha.

"They may take a little," said Mrs. Warren, "but the holes are too small for them. They're made for a bird's beak."

Tasha and Mrs. Warren waited by the window for a few minutes, but no birds appeared.

"Do you think it's broken?" asked Tasha.
This made Mrs. Warren laugh.
Soon Tasha was laughing too.

The next day, Mrs. Warren greeted Tasha with her finger on her lips.

"Shhh," she said. She led Tasha to the window. "Look."

Tasha looked out the window and saw a bright red bird on the feeder. She gasped. The bird cracked open a seed with its beak. The shell fell to the ground.

"That's a cardinal," said Mrs. Warren.

A bird with a black-capped head landed on the feeder.

"A chickadee!" said Mrs. Warren. Tasha smiled when she saw how excited Mrs. Warren was.

"All kinds of birds will come for seeds," explained Mrs. Warren. "If you put in just the striped seeds, you'll only get bigger birds."

"I'd like to see all the birds," said Tasha.

"Me too," said Mrs. Warren.

Tasha and Mrs. Warren watched the birds all afternoon. They were both surprised when Tasha's mother rang the doorbell.

"Is it five o'clock already?" Tasha asked.

CHAPTER 4 · TASHA'S GARDEN

For the remainder of the spring, Tasha and Mrs. Warren watched the birds gather around the feeder to eat each day. There was always something interesting happening.

One day, Tasha noticed a flower catalog on the sofa.

"I used to plant a garden for the hummingbirds," Mrs. Warren said. "I loved watching them."

"Why do they need a garden?" asked Tasha. "Can't they come to the feeder like other birds?"

"They might visit, but hummingbirds don't eat seeds," said Mrs. Warren. "Their beaks are meant to reach into flowers and drink nectar."

"It must be hard for Mrs. Warren to work in a garden," thought Tasha. Then she had another idea.

"Could I help with the garden?" she asked.

"But you're leaving for camp soon," said Mrs. Warren.

"Yes," said Tasha. "But I could still come over sometimes, if that's OK with you."

Mrs. Warren smiled. "Let's choose some flowers from this catalog," she said. "I'll order them today."

Tasha smiled back. She looked out the window again, but she didn't see campfires or pools.
She only saw the bright birds around the feeder and the space where their garden would grow.

NONFICTION · BIRD BEAKS

Written by Katherine Rawson

Chapter 1 | Bird Beaks 20

Chapter 2 | Hunters and Fishers 25

Chapter 3 | Sippers, Crackers, and Chisels 27

Chapter 4 | Some Unusual Beaks 30

CHAPTER 1 | BIRD BEAKS

There are many different kinds of birds. Some birds are small, and others are large. Some birds live in the water, and others live on land. Some birds sing, and others squawk or screech. But all of these birds have beaks.

Humans have mouths, but birds have beaks. Beaks are hard. They are made of **keratin**. Our fingernails and hair are made of keratin too.

A beak is an important tool. A bird uses its beak for eating and drinking. It uses its beak to build a nest and to **preen** its feathers.
A bird could not do these things without a beak.

All birds have beaks, but not all beaks look the same. Beaks come in many shapes and sizes.

This is a beak.

This is a beak too.

And so is this.

CHAPTER 2 HUNTERS AND FISHERS

If you look at the shape of a bird's beak, you may be able to guess what kind of food it eats. Some birds are **raptors**. They catch and eat small animals, such as mice, snakes, and even other birds. Eagles, hawks, falcons, and owls are all raptors.

A raptor uses its sharp beak to eat its **prey**. With its beak, a raptor can pull off feathers and fur. It can shred meat into bite-size pieces.

Some birds have beaks that are thin and sharp like spears. They are perfect for catching fish.

Terns and kingfishers have spear beaks. They fly above the water, looking for fish. When they spot one, they fly down and stab their dinner with their beaks.

Herons have spear beaks too. They stand in the water to feed. When a fish appears, they lean down and stab it with their beaks.

CHAPTER 3 SIPPERS, CRACKERS, AND CHISELS

A hummingbird's beak is long and thin like a needle. Hummingbirds stick their beaks deep into flowers and sip the **nectar**.

The sword-billed hummingbird has a beak that is longer than its body!

A cardinal has a cracker beak that is shaped like a cone with a groove on the inside. It can hold a seed on the groove and crack it open with its strong, hard beak.

A goldfinch has a cracker beak too.

A woodpecker uses its **chisel**-shaped beak to poke and peel off tree bark. If there are insects under the bark, the woodpecker picks them up with the sticky tip of its tongue.

Woodpeckers also use their beaks to make nest holes in trees.

CHAPTER 4 | SOME UNUSUAL BEAKS

Flamingo

A flamingo eats with its head upside down! A hungry flamingo will stick its head underwater. When it comes up, the water will pour out, but the tiny water creatures will stay in its mouth.

Toucan

Toucans love fruit. They pick it with their long, colorful beaks. The toucan uses its beak to reach fruit at the end of thin branches.

Pelican

A pelican has a pouch on its lower beak. The pouch is like a fishing net. The pelican uses it to scoop up fish from the sea. When the pelican closes its beak, the water drains out, and the fish stay in the pouch.

Like most birds, baby pelicans eat food that their mothers **regurgitate**. The mothers open their beaks, and the babies stick their heads inside to eat.

GLOSSARY

chisel
a metal tool that is flat on one end

keratin
a hard material that forms hair, nails, and beaks

nectar
the sweet liquid inside a flower

preen
to clean feathers

prey
an animal that is hunted

raptors
birds that hunt

regurgitate
to bring food from the stomach back to the mouth